D0908443

THE
KNOTT STORY

Cordelia and Walter on their wedding day.

Terry Tebbs

The Knott Story

From the Twentieth Century
Coined Commemorative Collection
of Great Americans

THE MARCHANT MINT LIBRARY

1992

Collector's Edition
First printing, April 1992

ISBN 0-916095-44-4

CONTENTS

Acknowledgements

Appreciation is given to the Knott family and their associates who patiently gave of their time in helping the author so much with this first volume.

I am also grateful to my family and those special friends who listened, persisted, encouraged and contributed.

To honor with hymns and panegyrics those who are still alive is not safe; a man should run his course and make a fair ending, and then we will praise him, and let praise be given equally to women as well as men who have been distinguished in virtue.

–Plato

Preface

$\mathbf{T}$his coined commemorative book is unique in format. Its purpose is simple and direct—to commemorate the lives of Walter and Cordelia Knott and to illuminate their character ethic.

Books are born in many different ways. The inspiration for this work was conceived on location at Knott's Berry Farm, Buena Park, California, early in 1991. The book's evolvement was a gradual process that found nourishment from many hours of study and reflection into the lives of Walter and his wife Cordelia.

"The Knott Story" is the first in a series of coined collectible editions that personify the spirit and character of those Great Americans of the Twentieth Century.

This collectible treasure not only captures forever the fascination of the Knott accomplishments, but also helps one better understand the passionate individual efforts required to make dreams a reality, and reflects the power behind their success.

Walter Knott Creed

Whatever we VIVIDLY imagine,

ARDENTLY desire,

SINCERELY believe,

and ENTHUSIASTICALLY act upon

must EVENTUALLY come to pass.

Walter Knott

THE
KNOTT STORY

Elgin C. Knott and Margaret Virginia Knott.
Walter's father and mother..

Chapter One

The Formative Years

Walter Knott was thrust into a man's role early. He was only six years of age when his father, Elgin, tragically and suddenly died. This untimely death certainly hastened Walter's maturity and he learned to accept responsibility at an early age.

Those early years, while formative, were very difficult. When the land bust of the 1890s cost the family their farm, Elgin's widow, Virginia Knott, and her two young sons, Walter and Elgin, purchased a small cottage on a sizeable lot in Pomona, California. This community, located about 25 miles east of Los Angeles, would be Walter's home during his boyhood.

Walter learned to love the soil when he was just a young boy. He loved to watch crops grow—especially his own. Sifting the soil through his fingers was exhilarating and while other boys his age were playing, Walter preferred to spend his time hoeing, raking and digging.

Even before his teens, Walter found meaningful expression by planting vegetable seeds in the family garden plot and carefully nurturing each plant to maturity.

His reputation as a successful young farmer spread throughout the town and he was able to convince other Pomona landowners to allow him to transform their weed patches into productive green gardens.

Selling his healthy produce was not difficult either, and the fruits of his efforts certainly helped augment the $6 each week his mother earned working six days a week, 10 hours a day, in a laundry.

Neither Walter nor his brother Elgin ever believed that they were poor. Both boys were taught early that there was "no free lunch," and that it was not only important, but necessary to be responsible.

As the "man of the family," Walter was always willing to share with his mother the money earned from selling his vegetables or the income earned working as the church janitor during his fifth and sixth grade years. He also delivered the local newspaper.

Elgin, too, did his share. He worked as an apprentice in a manufacturing company, and by the time he finished high school he was a journeyman machinist. He continued to work in this trade while attending a local university, and went on to become a professor of electrical engineering. He taught at Cal Poly (California State Polytechnical) San Luis Obispo for 38 years until his retirement.

It would be safe to say that Virginia Dougherty Knott made certain that her boys would be "failures at wasting time."

Walter continued to work with the soil throughout his teenage years. He became increasingly aware that he was a gifted farmer. Some how, he had been blessed instinctively with a "green thumb" and as he matured and grew, so did his success with nature.

His soul belonged to the earth and he proudly submitted to those whisperings that convinced him that when he sowed his seeds in fertile ground, he would be able to reap a harvest filled with endless bounty.

His affirmative attitude towards the field of farming was the impetus that pushed him out of Pomona to where he could gain additional experience and knowledge.

In this quest he left home, against the wishes of his mother, and headed east to California's vast, fertile Imperial Valley.

After working a season harvesting cantaloupes, he and his second cousin, Frank Cromer, rented a small piece of land in the arid but also rich Coachella Valley east of San Bernardino and Riverside and near the new town of Palm Springs. Here they planned to raise vegetables and market them in the towns nearby.

It was 1909 when these two young men broke soil. It wasn't long, however, until they realized that they were in trouble. Drought, a severe frost, and then a national economic depression forced Walter's cousin to find work elsewhere, leaving Walter alone to fight the elements and hopefully salvage some of their small investment.

Adversity in youth had trained Walter well. It had helped fashion his spirit. His winters of grief, his backbreaking hours of raking, digging, hoeing, and harvesting had all helped prepare Walter for this new and difficult challenge.

Long, lonely, diligent hours of labor did pay off and he was able to harvest his crops, market them and turn a small profit, not only for himself, but also for his cousin Frank.

WALTER'S
MOTHER EARTH

A loving father
    was laid to rest
And Walter wept
    in soft protest

He seemed so alone
    now fatherless
And felt he'd lost
    his youthfulness

On that dreary day
    he felt denied
He seemed so young
    and unqualified

Why was he called
    to lead so soon
He felt so confused
    that afternoon

He was only six
    his brother four
But a man he'd be
    he'd cry no more

This boy would take
    his father's place
He'd be the one
    to set the pace

This manly role
    would serve to train
Prepare him well for
    life's rough terrain

[15]

And as he grew
       he'd find a way
His mark he'd leave
       good deeds portray

He was a lover
       of the soil
His Mother Earth
       in it he'd toil

But work like this
       to him was play
Just like his
       favorite holiday

He'd find a lot
       that needed green
And with hard work
       he'd make it clean

Then carefully plant
    his seeds with care
For him they'd grow
    most anywhere

And when these tiny
    seeds would sprout
He'd sing a song
    then upward shout

His praise to God
    his Lord and King
Giving thanks to
    Him for everything

Yes, he knew from where
    all blessings flow
And his love to Him
    he'd always show

Cordelia Hornaday (now Cordelia Hornaday
Knott) taken about 1905.

Chapter Two

Cordelia Nostalgia

Walter always had praise for Cordelia. He loved his "Cordy," as he called her, and teamed together, they were a terrific force for good.

Cordelia Hornaday was born in Bushton, Illinois, January 23, 1890, daughter of John Hiram Hornaday of Ohio and Marion Lippencott Hornaday of Illinois.

In 1904 she moved with her father and sister, Rachel, to California. Her mother had recently died and the Hornaday family decided to make a new life in the West.

Cordelia enrolled in Pomona High School and she and Walter were classmates. Her soft green eyes, light brown hair and lively personality sparked a real interest in the shy and serious-minded Walter. They dated for five years and were married June 3, 1911.

Oscar Wilde said, "Men always want to be a woman's first love, women like to be a man's last romance." Wilde, a famous Irish playwright, poet and novelist, died in 1910, just a year before Walter and Cordelia were married, but his truism seemed to have been penned from their loving togetherness.

Cordelia said, "The best thing that happened to me was when I met my future husband, Walter Knott." To this Walter later responded, "If anyone was fortunate, it was I."

And Walter was fortunate. She made their first little home in Pomona a bit of heaven, and no matter what adversity or challenges they might face, she was there to offer loving support and encouragement.

One of Walter's early dreams was to homestead a ranch in the Mojave Desert; so he, Cordelia and baby Virginia moved there. But even the most creative efforts by the "miracle farmer" couldn't make the desert productive and profitable. There just simply was not enough water to grow the crops. Cordelia used to say, many years later, that the "only thing we were able to raise in the desert were children."

After three years they moved to Shandon, San Luis Obispo County, in Central California, where things weren't much better. Times were tough and uncertain, but somehow the Knotts survived. Daughter Virginia recalls, "Mother could always make something out of nothing." Cordelia earned $500 making candy by hand and selling it to buy the family's first Model T. It was this car which brought them to Buena Park, and the rest is history.

Walter, Cordelia and their children, Virginia, Russell and Rachael (Toni), came to Buena Park in 1920. A fourth child, Marion, was born there.

Cordelia had a wonderful way in the kitchen,

and although she said she'd never get into the restaurant business, she did.

On a Sunday in August 1934 at the early Knott's Berry Farm, Mrs. Knott served eight chicken dinners on her wedding china. The next day she served 10. As her "home cooking" fame grew, so did the lines that led to the tables, and now over 1.5 million chicken dinners are served each year at Knott's Berry Farm's Chicken Dinner Restaurant. In addition, thousands more are being served in the new Mrs. Knott's Restaurant and Bakery at locations outside Buena Park.

Cordelia was that "good woman behind a good man." Until her death on April 23, 1974, at age 84, she was an active partner in the family business, working right alongside her husband and family.

Former Sen. Barry Goldwater of Arizona paid tribute to Cordelia several years before her death, when he said: "She is a wonderful woman, a great addition, not only to womanhood, but to the citizenry of the United States, and she and her husband have contributed more, I think, than any two people I know to the good things of America."

CORDELIA

Her soft green eyes
    her loving ways
Her light brown hair
    her playful ways

Caused a response from
    a shy young man
And to her he'd give
    his own monogram

One that she'd treasure
    with all of her heart
As she pledged forever
    to do her part

She promised her all
    beside him she'd stand
And their talents combined
    she'd help them expand

A wife and a mother
    she committed to be
A pillar of strength
    for the world to see

And a prayer in her heart
    she'd always hold
Her faith and her strength
    were great to behold

And even in death
    her memory lingers on
Silently instructing
    all to carry on

Cordelia Hornaday Knott

Cordelia received a Happy Thanksgiving card from Walter in November 1964. Along with the sweet imprinted verse he penned in his own handwriting the following note to his loving wife:

Mother,

> *In thinking of the things I am thankful for at this Thanksgiving season I find I am thankful for you who has stuck with me for more than 53 years.*
> *You have always done your share and more.*
> *You have raised us a nice family that I am proud of and thankful for.*
> *You have helped mightily in building a business that I am thankful for and a little proud of too.*
> *I am thankful that we have so many things to be thankful for together.*

> *Thankfully yours,*
> *Dad*

Walter and son Russell assisting customers in early Berry Farm days.

Chapter Three

The Original Berry Farm

Knotts' Berry Farm, the nation's oldest and most popular, independently-owned themed amusement park, began as a simple berry stand on 20 acres of rented land along the rural roadside in Buena Park, California.

No one, not even Walter Knott, could have envisioned today's Knott's Berry Farm. "It could never have been designed," he said, "it just grew from year to year."

In 1920, when Walter moved to Orange County in Southern California, it was mostly farmland. Row after row of orange groves and walnut orchards lined the unpaved roads, while vast fields of beets and other lush green crops painted the area with the richness and beauty of a paradise.

To Walter it was a land of beauty and promise, and now nothing, absolutely nothing, would deter him from realizing his dream of successfully farming his own piece of ground.

In 1920, 30 year old Walter joined with his cousin, Jim Preston, creating a farming partnership. For $1,000 a year, they could rent 20 acres on a five year lease with an option to rent for another two years.

To the Knotts, who had spent three years trying to homestead in the Mojave Desert, it was like a golden opportunity to stake a claim on their own farmland.

Success, however did not come easily. Most of the family's savings went to purchase equipment and berry plants. The venture teetered on the edge of disaster for several seasons. The first year several heavy frosts—practically unheard of in Southern California—nearly wiped them out. The second year, berry prices plummeted.

Probably the only thing that saved the partners was Walter's tenacious spirit and his business acumen. He had been seasoned by adversity. Not only was he a gifted farmer, he had developed also the ways and means to market his produce. Even before the first crop came in, he was busy analyzing its future. He concluded he would get a better price for his produce if he marketed it himself. He put up a roadside stand to sell most of his crop of berries to the crowds of summer vacationers, who drove past the farm on Grand Avenue (now Highway 39, known as Beach Boulevard) on their way to Newport Beach and Balboa. The rest he would sell to local grocers and the Los Angeles Wholesale Market.

His was not the only berry stand along the highway, but his was always the busiest. Not only were his berries and other produce bigger and more delicious, but he also made certain that his were packaged and delivered to customers in fresh boxes and white paper along with a warm "thank you."

In his efforts to stay a step ahead of competitive berry stands, Walter wanted to produce and market an even better berry. In 1922, after two years of intensive searching, he learned through a newspaper article about a new berry called a "youngberry." This berry, a cross between a dewberry and a loganberry, was tastier and larger than other varieties and had been grown successfully in Citronelle, Alabama. Walter got the grower's address from the postmaster and ordered enough plants for a half-acre.

His partner, Jim Preston, expressed dismay at the project, but he shouldn't have worried. Walter played his experiment for all that it was worth, taking out advertisements announcing the new berries. Interest among seed merchants, growers and the general public was so high that the partners grossed more than $2,000 from that half-acre.

By now, the four Knott children tiptoed through the berry patches—Virginia, Russell, Toni and Marion. They picked berries and sold them at the stand, flagging down customers along the road. The family enterprise prospered until an oil boom in 1927 drove land prices sky-high.

The seven-year lease on the berry farm expired, and naturally Sam Coughran, the land-owner, wanted to sell while prices were high. It was either buy or move. Preston decided to withdraw from the partnership, move elsewhere and farm on his own where rent was cheaper. Walter couldn't see the point of walking away from such a growing and promising business, so he signed an agreement to purchase 10 acres at $1,500 an acre. Mr. Coughran agreed to forego a down payment, and Walter's dream of successfully farming on land that was his own now was a step closer to reality.

Now that the property was almost his, Walter decided to build a bigger berry stand, and behind it, a new home for the family. "Make a big kitchen, Walter," Cordelia counseled. "I'm going to can berries and jam, and make the finest pies that our customers ever sank their teeth into."

Walter liked that idea and suggested that maybe they should even open a restaurant. "No. I'll not go into the restaurant business," she stated. She

Walter and Cordelia Knott.

did agree to the addition of a tea room to serve customers, but refused to consider the idea of a restaurant.

The entire family sold pies and jellies, fruit and plants to ever-increasing crowds. But no matter how hard they all worked, Walter could not eke out enough to pay more than the interest charge on the land. They were not able to reduce the principle amount.

In 1929 the stock market crash threw even this delicate balance out of kilter. Now the cost of producing the fruit exceeded the price the family could get for it.

Friends encouraged Walter Knott to abandon the high priced land, default on his original agreement with the landowner, Mr. Coughran, and move to a plot nearby that could be bought for as little as $330 an acre. But Walter was a man of principle and his conscience would not allow him to do that. He decided to stay. Somehow, someway, faith, hope and hard work would sustain them.

THE KNOTT
FAMILY CREED

It was nineteen twenty
    in sunny Buena Park
When the Knotts arrived to
    work and make their mark

Battling with nature
    the earth they would subdue
Working together, they'd make
    their dreams come true

This family of Knotts,
    knit tightly, yes, they were
And nothing would halt them,
    depress them, nor deter

They vividly imagined
    and did ardently desire
Sincerely believing their
    dreams were set on fire

Their creed became a passion
    their dreams must come to pass
And with enthusiasm
    each one they would surpass

Their dreams were never-ending
    they never seemed content
And satisfying patrons
    was always their intent

And when their park you visit
    of this you can be sure
A promise of real value
    just like those days that were

Walter Knott, miracle farmer, inspects the boysenberries.

Chapter Four

The Boysenberry

The Great Depression that swept across the country in 1929 could have closed the door on the Knotts and their fledgling berry farm. It was a time of national economic collapse that would continue on through most of the 1930s. Businesses failed by the thousands, and hundreds of thousands of people could not find employment. Relief rolls swelled and standing in bread lines was a common sight.

Walter Knott knew the condition of the country. These were dark times, but he was determined; he was also schooled and conditioned. Circumstances would not defeat him. He was in love with his land. He loved to produce and his entire family followed his farming instincts.

Those instincts led him to moments of magic with berries, and it was his work with that fruit that not only kept the door to success open, but also widened that opening.

He was so well-known as an expert in berries by now that even the United States government came to him for help.

George M. Darrow, a representative of the United States Department of Agriculture, had heard of a remarkable new berry. Mr. Darrow was Chief of the Small Fruits Division for the USDA and he was anxious to learn more about this plant and its unusual bearing qualities. He wanted to know if Walter knew anything about this new berry, developed by a Mr. Boysen of Orange County, California.

Walter had never heard of Mr. Boysen or his berry, but when he learned that it was supposed to be a cross between a blackberry, a red raspberry, and a loganberry that turned out to be larger and more delicious than any of the parent stock, he became very interested.

A Rudolph Boysen was listed in the Anaheim telephone book. Superintendent of the city Parks Department, Mr. Boysen had experimented with the berry several years before, but he had abandoned it after no one seemed interested.

Walter and Mr. Darrow were interested, and they wanted to know if any of the experimental plants had survived. Boysen said he thought they had. Six plants had been planted in an orange grove he had sold some time ago.

Quickly the three men gained permission from the new owner to visit the grove. There, almost hidden among the weeds, were six scrawny berry vines, half-dead from neglect.

It was agreed that, with the landowner's permission, Walter would try to save the plants. He tended them carefully until spring, when he moved them to his berry farm's trial grounds. The new berries grew like the weeds that had surrounded them. Not only were the plants hardy, but the berries were enormous—bigger than a large man's thumb. As few as 25 berries filled a standard fruit basket.

The prodigy, named "boysenberry" after its originator, proved to be the superior berry Walter had been searching for. Sales soared. The boysenberry was in demand for canning, cooking and table eating, and other farmers ordered root stock as soon as it was available.

Walter felt a great deal of pride in helping other farmers survive the Depression by developing this new berry. As for Knott's Berry Farm, the nursery, berry salesroom and tea room had just about all the business they could handle.

The boysenberry, developed by Walter Knott, helped the Knotts and other farmers survive the great depression.

The Chicken Dinner Restaurant kitchen in the 1940s.

Chapter Five

The Chicken Dinner Restaurant

Cordelia had made it clear to Walter that she did not want to go into the restaurant business. She would not run a restaurant, but she would just serve chicken dinners. There would be potatoes and vegetables, but no selections—just chicken dinners.

Whatever they called it, in 1934 they were in the restaurant business. After that first day when they served eight dinners on their wedding china, the die was cast. These tasty chicken dinners were so good that by word of mouth the news spread quickly and in a few weeks they were swamped. The response was phenomenal.

A long line of people waited outside the 20-foot-square tea room at every meal. Good, inexpensive restaurants were hard to find, and word had traveled fast.

Walter and Cordelia agreed they couldn't keep people waiting, so they doubled the size of the room—and still the lines kept getting longer.

By August, they were serving 85 chicken dinners a day. In 1936, the Knotts added still more rooms and changed the name of the tea room to the Chicken Dinner Restaurant, but by the following year, the lines were so long that Walter, standing at the front door, could not see the end. People were waiting up to several hours for Mrs. Knott's chicken. While they waited, they bought berries, jams and pies to take home.

The Knotts decided to ask the bank for $10,000 to finance a major expansion of the restaurant. But when Walter approached his banker, the man rejected his request. "Restaurants are a notoriously bad investment," the banker said. Didn't Walter know that eight out of ten restaurants fail and the rate was even higher among restaurants located along highways?

Well, no, Walter hadn't known that, but he "was only trying to satisfy his customers, and ...." The money man waved his explanations aside. If Mr. Knott wanted to expand, the bank would be glad to lend him the money to expand his berry farm.

Crestfallen, Walter returned home to his family. That night the family council reached a unanimous decision. They'd expand more slowly and pay for the project as they went.

In 1937, the expansion was complete. In addition to the new dining rooms, there was a big kitchen separate from the family's quarters and a large parking lot with rows of trees. In a short time, the lines grew—but now the wait was shorter.

The restaurant opened on a year-round basis, and its fame continued to spread. On Thanksgiving Day 1937, it served 1,774 dinners.

Until her dying day 40 years later, Cordelia Knott insisted, "I'm not in the restaurant business."

Cordelia Knott filling one of her famous boysen-berry pies.

Mrs. Knott's famous chicken dinners are now available in California at the new Mrs. Knott's Restaurant and Bakery family restaurants.

Crowds flocked to visit Knott's Ghost Town.

Chapter Six

Ghost Town

Walter and Cordelia encouraged family members to consider themselves part of the team operating the farm, so when their children made suggestions, they were ready to listen.

The girls wanted to open little shops close to the restaurant. Virginia favored the idea of a gift shop, Marion and Toni eventually opened a clothing store, while Russell's efforts were directed towards the berries and the nursery.

In his 50th year, Walter took stock. The berry farm was succeeding beyond his wildest dreams, his family was grown and working with him in the business, but the country was still struggling to pull itself out of the Depression.

Walter had deep feelings of gratitude towards the early American pioneers. They were the ones who left their homes and traveled west across the Great Plains, deserts and mountains. They fought the elements and the Indians, subdued a continent and had done it without any help from the government.

He thought that people needed to be reminded of the pioneering spirit. His family could build something on the berry farm to be both a monument to the early pioneers—including his grandparents—and an educational diversion for people waiting to get into the restaurant.

"Those pioneers had something to teach us," said Walter. "People need to see how little they had to work with and yet how much they were able to accomplish. We decided to get a fine artist and do a big cyclorama (a painting with real objects in the foreground) of a wagon train crossing the desert. We'd build a town around it as a monument to those great Americans who opened up the West."

The first artist Walter commissioned labored for a year without achieving the desired effect. Then European artist Paul von Klieben took over the project and completed it within weeks. He also painted several portraits of Indian chiefs and a large mural for the new Steak House.

Von Klieben suggested bringing in actual old buildings to create a more natural atmosphere. That was all history-loving Walter needed to hear. The family concurred, and they found an old hotel built in 1868 near Prescott, Arizona, and brought it to the farm to house the cyclorama in 1940.

An authentic saloon soon followed, although, in keeping with the Knott's commitment to family values, no alcohol was sold anywhere on the premises.

In the next year, overtaken by collector's mania on a life-size scale, other buildings were added, including a jail complete with a "talking" inmate named "Sad Eye Joe," a Kansas school house, a blacksmith shop, and a picturesque collection of shacks from the Mother Lode territory. Covered wagons, stagecoaches, Boot Hill Cemetery

and employees dressed in authentic attire completed the effect.

Most of the buildings were authentic. Walter
took great care to preserve every bullet hole and
misspelled sign. The crowds loved it.

That same year, Walter had the opportunity
to see Knott's Berry Farm from the air. "We flew
over the farm, and I looked down on an awful
mess," he said later. He transformed the "awful
mess," which was the local dump, into Reflection
Lake. Von Klieben designed the adobe Chapel by
the Lake that overlooks it.

At the family's weekly business meetings, the
Knotts decided to continue expanding. Walter
summed up their feelings by saying, "We'll keep on
building as fast as we earn. We'll pay the help and
our taxes, and plow what's left back into the
business."

Between 1940 and 1955, Knott's grew into
a genuine tourist attraction. Visitors flocked to see
Ghost Town; the restaurants were surrounded by
successful shops; and Knott's Berry Farm jams and

jellies were packaged and sold throughout the
United States.

Ghost Town visitors can actually pan for gold and relive the gold rush days.

Ghost Town's first building: Walter Knott brought the Old Trails Hotel to Knott's Berry Farm from an abandoned town near Prescott, Arizona in 1940 to help entertain patrons of Cordelia Knott's Chicken Dinner Restaurant. It was the first of many authentic buildings which combined to create the Park's famous Ghost Town.

The Calico Railroad and the Butterfield Stage-
coach help create the atmosphere at Knott's Berry
Farm. Guests can take a journey around the
Farm and are subject to being held up by authen-
tic-looking robbers. Of course, it's all in fun.

Snoopy, the world's most beloved beagle, makes his home at Camp Snoopy, one of five themed areas at Knott's Berry Farm.

Chapter Seven

The Amusement Park

Gradually, Knott's Berry Farm began to change direction. Perhaps it was competition with Disneyland, perhaps the ideas of the younger generation, but a real train ride, a cable car and a gold mine where youngsters could pan for gold were developed. An electronic shooting gallery appeared, then a puppet theater, and finally a whole mountain was built to take six mine trains through a tour of a gold mine. Newspapers called the Calico Mine Ride, Knott's Berry Farm's "most adventurous undertaking." Independence Hall, a brick-by-brick re-creation of the country's most historic building—including a replica of the Liberty Bell—opened in 1966. Over the next few years, new rides appeared annually.

In 1968, the Knott family decided to fence the park and charge admission, a move many other amusement parks had made already.

The fence was a turning point. Before the fence, people came for the chicken dinner and browsed through the shops and attractions while waiting their turn in the dining room. But once they had to pay admission, patrons fresh from Disneyland expected to be entertained, which Knott's tried its best to do.

The $17 million capital investment required to do battle with the big corporate-owned theme parks drained the family pocketbook, but the Knotts had pulled through on less. Leadership of the family firm passed to the younger generation, as Cordelia died in 1974 and Walter involved himself in politics and humanitarian causes.

Under Marion Knott's supervision, some of the most significant expansion projects in Knott's Berry Farm's history were begun. Between 1968 and 1976, the park added its Log Ride, Fiesta

Village and Roaring '20s amusement areas. The Roaring '20s area—filled with such thrillers as the Gasoline Alley auto race, a 20-story parachute fall, and the Corkscrew roller coaster—was credited with improving park attendance 52 percent its first summer. Knott's Berry Farm pulled into third place in national attendance, behind Disneyland and Disney World.

After Walter's death in 1981, the family vowed to keep Knott's Berry Farm oriented toward families and education by offering a variety of attractions. And they have kept their promise. In 1983, Knott's allied itself with the world's most beloved beagle, Snoopy, and opened Camp Snoopy where smaller children could enjoy visiting with Charles Schulz's "Peanuts" gang. Four years later, the Kingdom of the Dinosaurs offered a realistic journey through the world of the prehistoric. Recently, the park unveiled the new Boomerang roller coaster, which takes riders upside down six times in less than a minute.

Things have changed since Walter Knott set

A 20-story parachute fall and the Boomerang roller-coaster offer park visitors exciting alternatives.

out to entertain the lines of people waiting for Cordelia's chicken dinners. Today Knott's sells 1.5 million of those chicken dinners a year. Annual attendance tops 5 million at the park, and at Knott's MarketPlace. But Ghost Town is pretty much the way Walter planned it, and the boysenberry jam is just as delicious.

Chapter Eight

Calico

Calico Ghost Town, located in the high desert just east of Barstow, California, was once a booming silver camp that yielded over $86 million worth of precious silver in just a little more than a decade. In its heyday during the 1880s, Calico was a bustling town of 3,500 people hustling to get rich quick. But when the high grade ore ran out and the price of silver dropped from $1.29 per ounce in 1880 to only 53 cents an ounce in 1896, the town quickly became deserted as the miners and business people moved on, abandoning their mine claims and leaving their homes and store buildings behind.

Walter was always looking for ways to

preserve the landmarks of the Old West, and Calico was especially appealing. His uncle, Sheriff John C. King of San Bernardino County, had grubstaked the miners that discovered the Silver King Mine in the Calico Mountains, and Walter had worked as a young man in the mines during the time he was homesteading with his young family in the nearby Mojave Desert.

Walter, his son Russell and artist Paul von Klieben visited the deserted mining camp. It was abandoned. Sagebrush now grew in the streets, what buildings still stood were crumbled and decayed and the old ore cars sat still on the rusty rails.

After walking the deserted streets and flying over the old camp, a decision was made to purchase the property. Contact was made with the Zenda Mining Company who held title to the mines and 70-acre townsite. The Knotts purchased the property and reconstruction began.

By 1966 the Knott family had invested over $700,000 in building and restoring the old camp to its original glory.

Walter's objective of preserving the colorful Calico history and spirit had been accomplished and in the fall of 1966, he and his family gave full title to all the buildings, land and artifacts to San Bernardino County.

Walter Knott and his family brought life once again to Calico. It does live again, and it is a permanent monument to the memory of those hearty men and women who battled the desert elements searching the hills for fortune.

The park system of San Bernardino County now owns and operates the historic town and it is a popular park attracting over a million visitors each year.

Inside Independence Hall at Knott's Berry Farm a 2,000 pound Liberty Bell proclaims liberty.

Chapter Nine

The Priceless Gift
of Freedom

Walter Knott was a truly great American.

He was blessed with the benefit of being born in the "Land of the Free," and this blessed feeling lived in his humble heart throughout his entire lifetime.

He was a simple God-fearing farmer who loved his family, his country and the priceless gift of freedom. Those things, coupled with a gritty, determined and tenacious spirit, enabled him and his family to build a living legacy that continues to propagate wholesome traditional values.

Walter had an intense determination to preserve and spread the cause and effects of freedom.

In the early 1960s, as maturing family members took over more and more responsibility in running the Farm, Walter was able to spend some of his valuable time and resources on fulfilling a dream that had been secretly growing in his heart and mind.

He was now politically active and was a powerful force in the community, personally proclaiming the cause of freedom.

His dream was to build on the farm an exact, full-scale, brick-by-brick replica of Independence Hall, shrine of American liberty located in Philadelphia.

Seventy-four year old Walter Knott vividly imagined, ardently desired, sincerely believed, and enthusiastically acted upon his dream and on July 4, 1966, Independence Hall at Knott's Berry Farm was dedicated and opened.

This historic building, just like the original

one, also housed a 2,000 pound Liberty Bell (yes, even with a duplicate crack)—one of America's greatest symbols of freedom.

In his dedicatory speech Walter reminded those in attendance that, "Over the years, millions of Americans will visit our Independence Hall and be reminded of our great American Heritage. Each year, thousands of school children will come and touch the Liberty Bell, and see where our great documents were signed."

Walter Knott believed that the 56 brave men who signed the Declaration of Independence and those who framed the Constitution of the United States were divinely inspired, and to them he was forever mindful of their great courage and willingness to sacrifice, even their lives, for the causes of freedom and liberty.

Walter said, "We are proud because the building of this structure took much effort, planning and saving. It was a dream we held for a long time before we could do anything about it. And we are humble as we stand before the building. It took

15 years to build the original Independence Hall, but the form of government which was conceived in that original building gave us an economic system which allowed this brick-by-brick reconstruction to be completed in seven months."

The completion and dedication of Orange County's Independence Hall stands not only as a witness to the value of freedom, but also serves as a monument to the greatness of those who built it.

Independence Hall at Knott's Berry Farm.

Russell, Marion, Toni and Virginia Knott inside Independence Hall.

The Knott family team: Virginia, Cordelia, Walter, Marion, Toni and Russell.

Chapter Ten

The Interdependent Knotts

The Knotts are principle centered people who live and teach the principles of creative cooperation.

While each member of the family is independent, Walter instinctively unified them, blending their individual talents together, forming a family team that became interdependent and highly successful. This cooperative family spirit of adventure, discovery and creativity became the catalyst in the amazing creation and growth of Knott's Berry Farm.

All four Knott children have been tremendous contributors and the farm provided the environment for each to unleash their own creative powers.

Virginia's Gift Shop, with "something for everybody at almost every price," was started by Virginia in 1939, with a table in the lobby of Knott's Chicken Dinner Restaurant.

Russell worked closely with Walter in business and management. Walter once said that it was with a great deal of satisfaction that he turned over the ever-increasing share of the overall management to his son. "It is gratifying to head a business and be able to leave so much of the detail to such a capable family," he said.

Encouraged by their father, Toni and Marion opened Marion and Toni's Fashions. The store featured custom-designed ladies apparel and today is still a popular place to shop.

Throughout the farm and in many different ways, members of the expanding family tree have been involved, each making his/her independent and unique contribution. The creation of Knott's Berry Farm was a family affair, and its continued growth will continue to be so.

Family partners meet monthly with President and Chief Executive Officer Terry E. Van Gorder and his crack management team to discuss new and even better alternatives, possibilities and opportunities. Even though Walter and Cordelia have passed on, their spirit remains, silently directing the forces and fortunes at Knott's Berry Farm.

Walter Knott, gifted farmer, business man and freedom fighter was a loving husband and wonderful father.

Cordelia Knott: Famous for her chicken dinners said she'd never be in the restaurant business.

John Wayne, close friend and frequent visitor, share a 1969 event with Walter at Knott's Berry Farm.

Chapter Eleven

Walter Knott
'To Know Him Was
To Love Him'

Walter Knott passed away on December 3, 1981, eight days before his 92nd birthday.

He was one of those rare individuals who invested his time, his energy and his resources in doing good. The fruits from his labors are abundant and obvious; they seem almost infinite and will certainly outlast us all.

Walter was also a gifted farmer who developed his God-given talents. As he sifted the soil through his fingers he dreamed, and those dreams, nurtured by a simple value system, turned a modest roadside business into the nation's most popular independently-owned family theme parks.

But he did lots more. He was also a fearless pioneer and patriot.

After his death, the following editorial appeared in the "Fullerton Daily News Tribune." "When President Ronald Reagan, then governor of California, presented Walter Knott with the 1968 Free Enterprise Man of the Year Award, he said of him: 'Walter Knott is one of America's great patriots; one who has successfully climbed to the very top rung of the ladder of success, as few Americans have; yet one who has always been careful to see that he left each rung of that ladder in good repair so those who followed after would have less trouble in climbing life's ladder than he, Walter Knott, California's and America's Great Pioneer/Patriot.'

"Walter Knott, who died that Thursday at his beloved Knott's Berry Farm at the age of 91, was certainly that—a pioneer and a patriot.

"He rose—truly struggled—from the simplest

pioneer beginnings to a position of eminence and fame, transforming his small nickel-a-basket berry stand in Buena Park to California's second largest tourist attraction.

"His name was synonymous with patriotism. If anyone could be called a fierce patriot, it was Walter Knott. Knott's Independence Hall stands as a monument to his love of his country. But more than that, his philosophy of life was dedicated to a strong belief in the same principles that motivated the nation's Founding Fathers, the men who wrote the Declaration of Independence and the Constitution.

"He was a pious man, a humble man who believed that, as he put it in a speech not many years ago: 'Freedom rests, and always will, on individual responsibility for each of us, and does not rest in civil rights, government or in the hands of powerful politicians. It rests with you and me.'

"Men of Walter Knott's stature and philosophy are a rarity in this 20th century. North Orange County was fortunate to have this pioneer and patriot pass this way." **(Editorial reprinted by permission from the Fullerton DAILY NEWS TRIBUNE.)**

Walter Knott lived a simple life and he asked that his funeral services be conducted in the same way. In a written request he said: "Make the whole thing simple, friendly and happy. Why should it be otherwise? Life has been good to me and death is a great adventure. The greatest adventure of a very full life."

As requested, the graveside services were attended by members of the immediate family and a few close friends only. There was no public or memorial service.

Draping the coffin was a U.S. flag which had flown over our nation's capitol on December 4, 1981, the day after his death. It was presented to the Walter Knott family in his memory by North Carolina Sen. Jesse Helms.

Flags in Buena Park were flown at half-mast, and bells on the farm were rung at 10 a.m. concurrently with the funeral services.

Tributes to Mr. Knott were numerous. As

word of his death was received, friends throughout the nation wrote, wired or called to express their sorrow and to praise him for his life-long achievements, high ideals and patriotism.

A Great Loss

"It's a great loss of a great American," said Buena Park Mayor Jesse Davis, who added, "we're proud that Buena Park was the home of Mr. and Mrs. Knott."

Arizona Sen. Barry Goldwater, another long-time admirer, said: "Walter Knott was one of the most dedicated, honest Americans I have ever known and his examples. . . to those of us who followed, will forever be in the best interest of our way of life."

Orange County Supervisor Bruce Nestande said, "Walter was the last of the real pioneers. His grandmother and mother came across the country in a covered wagon, he worked in the mines in Calico and it all culminated in a deep love for America and its traditions."

Just a Farmer

Dean Davisson, who worked in Public Relations at the farm for 18 years, said Mr. Knott never had a business card. "He just identified himself as a farmer.

"On the wall in my office is Mr. Knott's success formula," said Dean. "It says, 'Whatever we vividly imagine, ardently desire, sincerely believe, and enthusiastically act upon must inevitably come to pass.'

"If he ever had a fault it was that he was too generous with his time and money," Dean added.

Carol Ardrey, Mr. Knott's personal secretary the last 11 years, before his death, said: "To know and work with Mr. Knott has been the greatest privilege of my life.

"Anyone who met him came away a better person for having known him—with his example of quiet determination, strength and courage, gentleness and love, and a constant concern for the welfare of others. I can truly say, 'to know him was to love him.'

"Many of Mr. Knott's nurses came to work as young girls and they would say, 'Our parents raised us, but Mr. Knott formed us. Our character, values, principles—those things of lasting value that will be a part of us—we got from him.'" Carol added.

A Giant of His Age

Newspaperwoman Ann Terrill wrote: "Walter Knott was a giant of his age and the last of his kind in these parts."

"He was truly a great gentleman whom Orange Countians, and indeed the world, will mourn. He gave us so much pleasure it is difficult to think of sadness in the same context with Walter Knott," said Sheriff Brad Gates.

Buena Park Councilman Ken Jones said, "Mr. Knott was an outstanding gentleman. A fine, outstanding humanitarian."

An editorial in the "Orange County Register" said: "Orange County—indeed, the world—lost a legend last week in Buena Park. The man is gone. He left the world a little better than he found it.

Rest in peace, Mr. Knott."

Guy Tester, who worked at the farm for 33 years said, "Mr. Knott was a man who never asked anything of anybody else. He did for others almost constantly, yet he never asked anything for himself. Everything he did was for the good of the country and for the good of his fellow man.

"The thing that always impressed me," continued Guy, "was Mr. Knott's humility. And the man with a lot of money never got any more attention from Mr. Knott than the man who was broke."

Norm Emerick, Knott's Graphic Arts Department, agrees. "If you had a complaint, Mr. Knott always said his door was open. You'd just walk in and sit and talk with him 'till your problem was solved. No one was too small to come in and talk to him."

Always Right

Bud Hurlbut, with whom Mr. Knott built many of Knott's rides, said, "Mr. Knott was one of the finest men I ever knew. He was a genius when it came to deciding where a ride should go. He'd look over a site, put his heel down in the corner and say 'measure from here.' And he was always right."

The Los Angeles County Board of Supervisors adjourned their weekly meeting in honor of the memory of Mr. Knott and were sending a resolution to the Knott Family in his honor.

There were so many more tributes that it is impossible to list them here. Mr. Knott would feel honored and undeserving as he considered himself just a simple farmer. "Growing food is just as important as any work," he'd say.

Greatest Tribute

Perhaps the greatest tribute to the outstanding character of Mr. Knott is the replica he built of Independence Hall—the fulfillment of his life-long dream. He had a fierce determination to preserve the ideals upon which this country was founded.

"I would rather leave to my family the freedom from fear, the opportunity to go as far as they have the ambition and the intelligence to go, and their freedom than to leave them all the money in the world," said Mr. Knott.

We Are Now Keepers
of the Flame
By TERRY E. VAN GORDER,
President & CEO of Knott's Berry Farm

Although Walter Knott has bidden farewell, the Flame of integrity, decency and humanity that he kindled at Knott's Berry Farm and nurtured here down through the years remains with us today. We are now the Keepers of the Flame. Knowing of the pride, the courage, the dedication and love with which Walter Knott hand-sculpted the essence of his Farm, we are compelled by natural respect, privilege and inspiration to ensure that his Flame will glow, as it did while he was here.

Great and rich is our legacy from Walter

Knott. His presence shall ever be throughout the Park, for his calloused hands carved the very atmosphere and medium through which we live and work and entertain. With hard work and brilliant simplicity, he caringly introduced water and life to this once dusty plain. Lovingly, he caressed the earth and watched her reproduce—not only the boysenberry, magnificent trees and beautiful flowers but, more importantly, the taproot of a most worthy and enduring institution.

It takes little imagination to see him still, pacing off across Fiesta Village, digging his heel into the rich berry farm soil within which he had mixed such a great portion of himself for more than six decades and, turning to Bud Hurlbut, owner of Hurlbut Amusement Company, saying: "The center of the merry-go-round goes here." That's the way he did it. Such was the measure of the man.

The mark of Walter Knott's character and personality is everywhere at Knott's. It is a hallmark of truth and honesty, wisdom and common sense, pride and self-reliance, hard work and perseverance, love and dignity, piety and gentleness, faith and simplicity.

How fortunate are we that we may continue the work and the dreams that Walter and his beloved Cordelia Knott pioneered. And how many Americans today can pass their hours of contribution in an atmosphere so dedicated to the America that is everybody's dream...and Walter Knott's reality.

Walter Knott's sense of history blessed him with an even greater sense of future. We shall not fail, for his Flame shall ever light and warm the way. Let us now commit ourselves to understand and love the Flame—that we may truly be the Keepers. May we seize upon the inspiration inherent within this moment of time and let the Flame enhance our spirits and lead the way to a future bright with promise and happiness.

Most of the copy for this chapter was reprinted by permission from a supplement to the Dec. 11, 1981, Knott's Berry Farm employee newsletter, "The Berry Vine," by Patsy Marshall, editor.

Paul Bunyan will stand tall at Knott's Camp Snoopy, the centerpiece of the Mall of America in Bloomington, Minnesota.

Knott's
Camp Snoopy
Bloomington, Minnesota

The Knott's Berry Farm entertainment park in Buena Park, California was founded by Walter Knott and his family. It is the nations most popular independently owned family theme park.

In the Fall of 1992, Knott's Berry Farm will bring a $70 million indoor family theme park to Mall of America, the nation's largest shopping center located in Bloomington, Minnesota.

The new indoor theme park will feature rides, entertainment, Snoopy and the Peanuts Gang and is the company's first venture outside of Southern California.

This new family wonderland will not only entertain millions, but will also lend further credance to the Knott legacy. Imagination does rule and the deeds of yesterday are but today's memory while tomorrow brings opportunity for today's dreams.

A PSALM OF LIFE

Lives of great men

all remind us

We can make our

lives sublime

And, departing, leave

behind us

Footprints in the

sands of time

Henry Wadsworth Longfellow
1807-1882